SHADOWS

&

REFLECTIONS

ILLUSTRATED VERSE
IMAGINED OR REMEMBERED

by Sam Wharton

Burlington, Vermont

Onion River Press
89 Church Street
Burlington, VT 05401
info@onionriverpress.com
www.onionriverpress.com

ISBN: 978-1-966607-35-9

Library of Congress Control Number: 2025922632

To the memory of
Roger Nye Lincoln
(1916-2004)
&
Nancy A. J. Potter
(1926-2023)
Both of whom encouraged me to write.

*With thanks to my mentors,
I share a collection of poems that have
been inspired by or have inspired my
drawings, paintings and photos.*

IMAGINING
MY
FATHER

IN THE SUMMER OF 1946

I was nearly four and playing in a place I called 'the soft sand.'
The soft sand was a small wash where the gentle slope of my grandmother's driveway,
U-shaped, leveled off.

Over time and whenever it rained, the sand sifted down through an up-slope of pea stone
and pebbles and fanned out in a flat expanse.
There, with my red model tractor, I tilled imagined farmland.

The tractor had two big wheels spread apart in the rear
and two tiny ones tightly centered in front.
Together they rutted roadways in a powdered terrain.

My hand fit perfectly on the slim body of my tractor.
As I was about to roll a path to a house I had crafted with carefully piled flat rocks,
I heard the crunch of much larger tires on the rise above.

The coloring book car's chrome front sparkled.
Bright yellow metal bubbled around the wheels, and
arched to rim the windows and a pair of great green doors.

In graceful unison, the doors swung open, and four strangers...
men in uniform...three from the back seat and one from the front,
stepped onto a brightly crayoned page.

Except for the guy who emerged from the driver's seat,
whose garb was garishly hued to match the car,
their suited colors were muted.

The others were a collective
of tan and brown with, maybe, some muted green.
These were three of my lead soldiers come to life.

The tallest of the three wore a hat with a shiny brim reflecting
a brass medallion and rising to a backward tilting, neat, round surface.
This man was to become my demanding, crosspatch grandfather.

In the middle swaggered the shortest of the three.
Curly black hair twisted from under a narrow pointy cap jauntily shoved to one side.
He was my mother's brother and would become my uncle.

The third, a man with a hat like my grandfather's but with its sides tugged down.
That distortion was a pilot's 50 mission crush...
The head beneath...I later learned...had been my father's.

The driver was the only one to smile. His green brimmed hat was yellow.
He cruised at a different level, but the cap, in cabby caricature, sported
The 50 mission crush.

The three in khaki and olive drab had been away at war and barely knew me.
They absently waved, marched out of the driveway,
up the front steps and into Mima's house.

I waved, but at the cab driver, who,
as he drove by, grinned and, from the brim of his cocked hat,
flipped me a two-fingered salute.

The dust settled, and I went back to work on the approach to my stone farmhouse.

IN THE SUMMER OF 1946...A FOOTNOTE

My brother, my Irish Twin, has no memory of such a moment and to this day taunts me about the improbability of my recollection. In my mind, the occurrence is real, and I have no memory before or beyond that cartoon moment. He would fly away again, and we would not see him for another ten years.

Who was this guy, where had he been, and where did he go? The questions would echo and my response to those queries would be based upon limited and somewhat ephemeral resources.

I do remember those thousand-piece jigsaw puzzles. During Christmas week there would always be one dumped out on a card table in the den at Mima's house. We weren't supposed to take hints from the image on the box, but the carton was on a bookshelf nearby. And now and then glances that way provided some helpful hints.

The pieces that comprise my father's life and character are, however, scattered on a multi layered, semitransparent surface. And...there is no box on a nearby shelf. The pieces, some imageless on both sides, are flipped and turned. The corners and edges are missing.

Where is the top? Where is the bottom? Where are the bounding sides?

Lacking these reference points, I would need to frame an image from tales told or overheard, from letters found in shoe boxes, from deckle edged photos corner held in musty albums, and from, mostly, unfocused recognitions and recollections.

I know that his father had left him.

Maybe, he, too, had felt the confusion of being lost or left behind.

Maybe he and I were like the balls that roll into the tall grass beyond the mown lawn: not so much lost as not yet found. Perhaps, if I imagine his past, his world and his travels, I can color the blank pieces, form the edges, and create a bounded image that rolls the balls...us...out of the weeds and onto the fresh cut grass.

IMAGINING MY FATHER

I was a baby when he,
Bound for the Hump,
Boarded a bomber
And flew away.

And I imagine him winging:

To

Dinner in Bermuda,
Lunch in the Azores, and
Supper with Ingrid in Casablanca.

By

At dawn, the
Bedrock Sphynx, and
Stone stack Pyramids.

Over

High above
The Taj Mahal and
Agra's armored Onion dome.

Atop

The Third Pole and into China
To sing, wing tip to wing tip,
With Gene Autry.

REACH AND RUN:
MY FATHER HEARS THE SIREN'S CALL

Float or Fly
Reach and Run
Pitch and Yaw

I loose the painter.
Or...
Kick out the wheel chocks.

I unfurl the sails.
Or...
Ease back the stick.

I run free before the wind.
Or...
Unburdened, rise into it.

Awash or aloft
I am untroubled,
In control,
Alone...
In my element.

Then, inevitably, I feel Her.
First...a hint, a tail wind:
Aura the Windmaid.
Then She appears,
Floating, barely demure:
Scallop saucered Venus.

I come about.
Or...
Touch down.

At first I am happily grounded.
She is my water and air.
Her smile, her laugh, the curve of her, a toss of her hair...
Love, momentarily, thrilling as wing and sail.

Always charming, and showing my best side,
Here, too, I man the helm or hold the wheel.
The movement around, in and through her is:
Water licking a tapered bow!
Wind caressing a quivering airfoil!

We float and fly; move as one.
I read the tide lines and sail on.
I intuit the streamlines and fly ahead.
And we course our own sea and sky.

But…

She wants to draw
Tidelines as timelines,
Confine and define us
In the tug and pull of her lunar cycle.

She luffs the sails and damps the wing lift.

I loose the painter.
Or…
Kick out the wheel chocks.

I unfurl the sails.
Or…
Ease back the stick.

Soon, a diminishing figure
On the dock.
Or…
By the runway,

She shrinks away in my wake.
Or…
Back in my slip stream.

Untethered, I sail and soar; tack and barnstorm
Toward the next She…
And the next,
And…

LOOKING...AND READY
TO FLY OR SAIL...
AWAY

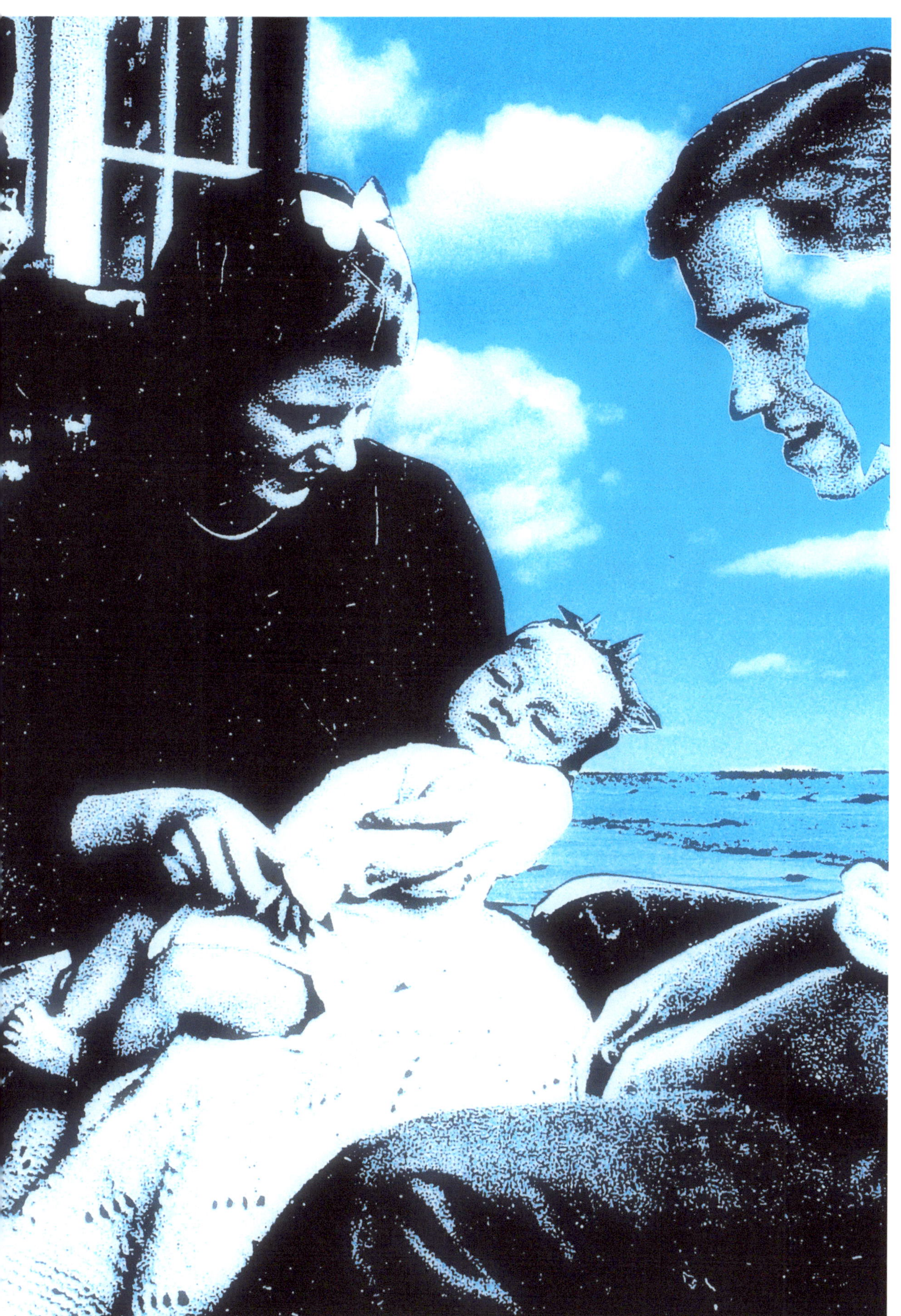

LOVE ADRIFT

He could soar and sail.

I cannot fly,
Nor man the helm.

But...In Love

Recurrently drawn
To scented breezes
And warm offshore eddies.

Aloft and asea in widening gyres,
Wayward, too...

I am my father's son.

I KNOW IT'S CRAZY

I wanted to be Holden Caulfield
In a big field...
On the edge of some crazy cliff
Catching thousands of little kids
But...
Too often
I behaved like Rabbit Angstrom,
Heart gone hollow,
In a vacant field of cinders,
And...

Failed to catch my own

GROWING UP AND KID'S STUFF

THE THIRD FLOOR

The tall house
Wore a slate faced,
Squared up,
Mansard hat,
and…
As a boy,
I lived just above its guttered brim.

My brother and I shared
An illustrated room…
A Wonderland…
With painted on:
Alice, Humpty,
The Walrus,
The Carpenter, and
The odd ambler clams
In their laced-up shoes.

I wondered then,
And I wonder still:
Just who tied and bowed
The odd ambler clams'
Laced up shoes?

CHRISTMAS PASSED

On New Year's Day,
I was nine, maybe, ten.
Maury's dad wore speed skates.
I couldn't see them,
but I could hear the long flat blades
carving and shaving the pond ice ahead.

He towed us.
A sled train with
Runners chattering,
mittened hands clinging to ankles;
mine around my brother's,
his around Peggy's,
hers around Johnny's,
his around Maury's.

I was at the snapping end of a careening whip.
I thought about the TV cowboy
Lash LaRue.
He could undo a bandit's gun belt
and disarm an outlaw with a flick of his bullwhip.

My waggling arc was aimless.
I snapped.
I skittered,
snapped, again,
lost a mitten,
and inflexibly flipped my Flyer.

Just before I slept,
I saw my breath...cumulus
on a blue winter sky.

When I opened my eyes in semi-dark…
first the one not held shut by the couch cushion,
then, with a painful turn, the other…

I could see
the procession.
Carved camels and kings
on their way across the bookcase
to kneel at the manger.

But tall silhouettes were dismantling the Christmas tree.
Bubbles still boiled up in tiny glass spires,
but…
the glass orbs were missing.
Their convex reflective world no longer shone.

"What are you doing?
We never had Christmas!"
The magi and their mounts
were wrapped and smothered
in suffocating wads of cotton.

The plug was pulled.
The bubbles continued for a while,
but, their magic had been exposed.

It was all just
methylene chloride
and
heat from incandescent light…

Just before I slept,
I saw my breath…cumulus
on a blue winter sky.

WE'LL JUST GO

Mary was crying.
I wasn't sure why, but I knew
Her father made her cry.

We sat at the base of the birdbath;
Home den for hide and seek.
Our backs to her house,
I faced south and squinted into bare branch, back-lit woods.
Her shoulder next to mine,
She faced east and sobbed to the road at the end of her driveway:

"I want to go."
"We could, you know...We could go."
 Most days I walked to her house.
 I easily walked to her house.
"I'll come, and we'll just go."
 She hid her eyes and sniffed into prayer posed hands,
 Wiped her nose on her sleeve,
 Nudged me as she spun out from under
 Our concrete umbrella, and

With a wave, ran...
Away into porch shadow.

On a cold night threatening snow,
I determined to take her away.

We'd be hungry by morning, so...
In my uncle's black lunch box:
A plaid thermos of cold milk, and my scout knife
To carefully cut the flaps and waxed paper around Frosted Flakes:
The little box became a bowl.

I slept in my snowsuit and leggings.
No boots...too much noise.
A blue white moon lit me lacing PF flyers...

Rubber soles on rubber treads,
No squeak no creak.
I crept down the back way.

The door at the landing swung open.

"Where do you think you're going?"
My rumpled grandfather growled.
I straightened, showed him the lunch box,
And told him I was running away with Mary.

"Do you know what time it is? Go back to bed!"

I went back to bed.

Whenever her father called,
Mary turned to the road at the end of her driveway.

FILMSTRIPS

When I was a kid,
Sometimes...
They taught us stuff
With...
Filmstrips.

Really! Strips of film
With...
Light bulb projected times and places,
And...
A voice on a scratchy LP

Droning through
Giza...
The Pyramids: King Tut lies here.
Beep...
Agra, Uttar Pradesh

Beep. Move quickly on
To...
Greece, Rome
Or...
The hot bulb burns and bubbles the Taj Mahal.

When I was a kid,
Always...
My times and places were framed in short filmstrips.
Never...
Coherent or feature length.

DUCK AND COVER

We sat at our desks.
Behind us the projector chattered.
On the screen, black and white,
In a flash, a wooden house splintered.

When you hear the siren,
Get into the hall.
Stay away from windows and doors,
Or dive under your desk and cover your head.

On Saturday or Sunday
Alone at the playground,
No siren, no hall, no desk to dive under.
In a flash, I and the swing set vaporize to

Shadow play on blast bleached brick…

A red skateboard,
Wheels still spinning,
Shimmers…
In complementary
Roadside green
And
Misses the boy
Launched into the
Blue.

NEXT IN

The turners turned
The braided arc
Tap-tapped
The summer street.

Next in…
On tiptoe,
Carol bobbed and sang

"Lemon and lime
Be on time
Don't be late
Be on time."

Next jump in…

Next in Carol,
Shadow too tall,
Kept time and
Changed the tune:

"Sorry, Sorry
I have no time."

At jump rope pace
She ran for home.
Bound the steps and
Hopped the railing.

Just in time.

The Caddie,
A pale blue pond
On an arborvitae shore,
Shimmered, whirred, and ticked
Like the rope on the street.

Daddy waved.

Carol jumped in.

SALLY LOST AND FOUND

I saw him through my glass front door.
A neighbor boy graced my steps, knocked and asked:

"Have you seen Sally? Um…our dog.
She is big, soft, and black, and
we can't find her."

I turned on the porch light, and on the steps
I put a bowl of the little I had that a dog might eat…
A crust of bread and bits of leftover grilled chicken.

The boy returned.

In a couch corner, curled under a comforter,
Sally had been found.

He smiled and extended his hand my way.
In it, black-dotted and green italic, was a small white box.
"I hope you like Junior Mints."

In a small child's palm,
Sweet thanks given…shared joy…
For love found, not lost.

TVILLINGER

When I reach for her,
her hand balloons to nearly
touch my own.

When I talk,
she nibbles and mutely
parrots my every word.

She only listens.

Never a challenge...no rebuke.
At the edge of a golden orb,
face to face I meet...my twin in
the polished doorknob.

EVER YOUNG

Across a tiny bench
on branch held
ropes...

Descendpullbackkickout
and arc
earth to sky.

A pendulum of
arms, legs
and flying hair.

Ever young
We swing,
Toy with

And
Know not...
Gravity

I FOUND MY BROTHER.

The car was running
The windows were closed

His cheeks were rose lit
His broad chest still.
I tapped the glass.

Lost in thought, it seemed...
He gazed
Across the azure sound.

Today...
All thoughts lost,
The spotted eagle ray
Will swim back and forth
And wonder...

Where is my friend?
And the calico clams he digs for me?
Will no one gently grasp my shouldered wings
And ride with me to Flatts and back?

No one will.

In his breathless room,
Shuttered and still...
I see his Airplane models
Threaded from the ceiling
Spin and swirl.
On the sound at reef's edge,
The ray breaches and flies.

He is here... I Found My Brother.

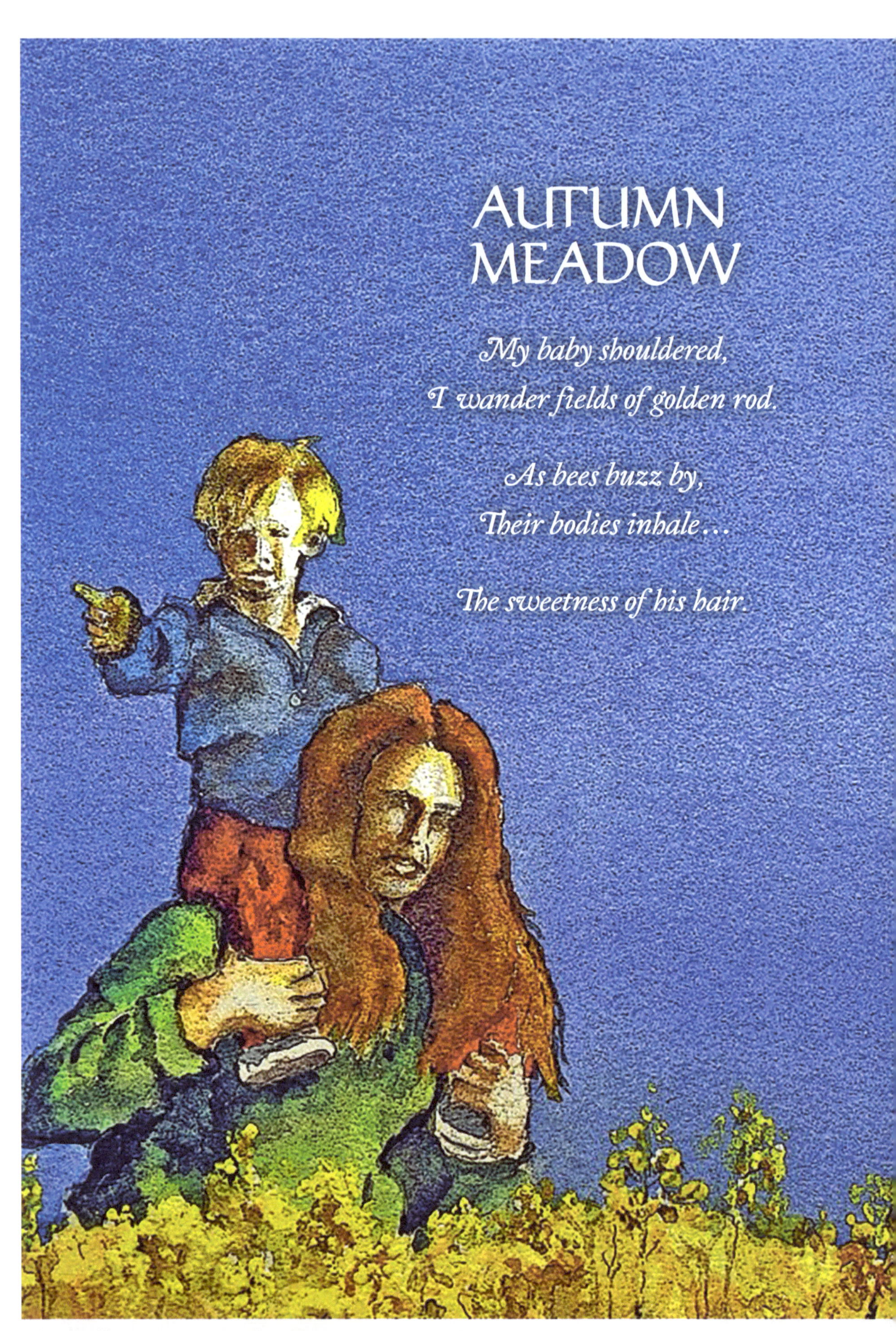

AUTUMN
MEADOW

My baby shouldered,
I wander fields of golden rod.

As bees buzz by,
Their bodies inhale…

The sweetness of his hair.

WHAT FRIENDS ARE FOR

Where we lived was
new to my eight-year-old.
He struggled to
To fit in.

On an early evening walk
sunset shone a sandy bank,
glinting the neck of a bottle
with a white porcelain stopper.

What a find.
I dug it out, and
The trail side dune avalanched
Sand cached ancient decanters.

Arms full,
I showed them to my neighbor.
Her eyes brightened.
She smiled and said:

Put the them back
Let your little boy find them.

I did.
He did
And began to make
A new place his own.

THE
OLD
BALLGAME

WE SAW IT ON THE RADIO

The War was over.
The sands of Utah Beach
Shaken from my uncle's hair.

Now...no M-1
With a shovel he widened Route 1,
Came home, shook off roadbed grit.

And asked:

Mother, how'd my Yankees do today?

My Mima and I spent
Our afternoons beside the radio,
We knew, and she said:

They won six to nothing.
Mr. Rizzuto had a single and a double.
Mr. Berra and Mr. DiMaggio each hit homeruns.
Mr. Raschi struck out eight Tigers.

A few years later,
She rode in an elevator with Mr. Berra.
My eyes widened.
Did-ya get Yogi's autograph?
No dear, we talked about opera.

Now I go to games with my grandson.

I wish my Mima were here.

She would meet Theo,
Tune us in
And...in full Coloratura
We could sing to her of
Mr. Jeter, Mr. Guidry and Mr. Judge.

GIVE IT A RIDE

Pink gum dust blown away
the sky framed Golden Boy,
bat to shoulder,
is on my bike.

And

to clothes-pinned rounds of
card to spokes applause,
The Mick and I go…
out of the park.

A BALL IN PLAY

Back in the '60s
I took my little brother
to a Yankee game.

He was ten.
"Hey, should I bring my glove?
Might snag a foul ball."

His fist taps the pocket
"Nah, don't both…"
I stopped mid-sentence.

It had never worked for me,
but he is just starting.
"Yeah, sure, bring it."

Outside of the stadium,
he dances ahead,
pounding his glove.

Leaping through a season's worth of
windblown dust and popcorn fragments,
he snags an airborne paper cup.

He crumples the Dixie,
tosses it my way and shouts:
"I'm gonna snag one!"
We make our way past
the odd salt shaker ticket booths and
through the gates behind home plate

And are ushered to
field level seats
on the third base side.

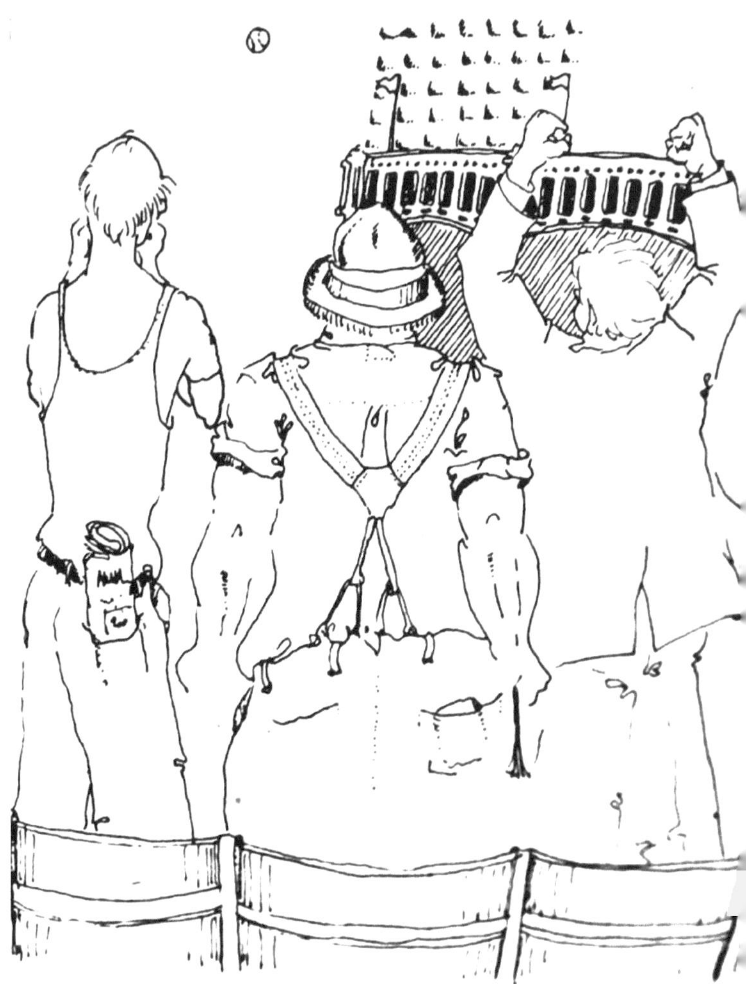

The game is a three-inning event.
Mantle goes yard in the second.
Yogi homers...last time ever...in the fourth.

But real History is made.
in the third...
field level seats, third base side.

With Boyer on second,
Drabowski delivers a fastball...outside corner.
Kubek swings a tad late and an inch low.

Off the bat, the ball
arcs high over the visiting dugout
and heads down.

My beer and scorecard are
strangely transported...and join
the pencil in my throwing hand.

This ball imprinted with Joe Cronin's
has my name on it, too.
Sensing my moment, people fan away.

Gathering speed, a white, red stitched blur,
the ball smacks into my cupped palm.
I hand it to my brother.

For a few years,
the ball was displayed
on a shelf in his bookcase.

It stood on a pedestal,
which had been
the cardboard core of a toilet paper roll.

It's gone now.
Lost in the woods.
Whacked away in a backyard game of Fly's Up.

Sometimes when I visited my Mom,
I'd drift into the ferns and trees and
kick and scuffle the undergrowth,

Keeping an eye open for
fragments of red thread and
brown tongues of horsehide.

And

Remembered the catch,
the impact, the shivering journey down my arm to
the gum card center of me.

FLORA AND FAUNA

THROUGH A WINTER WINDOW

A cardinal couple:

She,

close by, tawny tinted.

He,

Field's edge and bright beyond,

Finds a seed…A tiny gift…

And

Returns to her.

Across the room,

I wonder…

How would you like your toast?

LAST LEAF

Atop a tiny maple

Crests a golden compliment…

…A final taunt…

to

The blue-gray flood of wintertide.

THE BUTTERFLY EFFECT

Long ago, fifty autumns gone,
Checked and paint spattered
Two by twelves bridged
A run of rusted roof jacks.

The kid and I
Set "TIT"
And "BANG"
Drove fat head nails
Just above the illusionary,
Die cut loops.

As we nailed,
Black asphalt shingles
Lapped over the course beneath
And crept up to cover
Tar paper folded over
The roof peak.

Beyond the ridge
To the East and West…
We could see the bridges.
The entire westward span;
And tower tops to the east.

Cabled steel and cement,
It seemed,
Kept our island from
Following the waning summer
On a drift south
And out to sea.

Roof jacked and warmed,
Sun on the black 10/12 pitch
"TIT-BANG"
We buttoned up
Against the inevitable
Slant of sleet and snow.

The kid went down
For another bundle.
My hammer clawed to a partially set nail,
I reclined,
My back sloped 10/12,
And rested.

The kid didn't dump the bundle.
He cradled it,
And,
Baby to crib, gently
Set it on the plank.

"Look," he said.

I sat up and looked.

Stenciled black on through lit orange,
On the butt of my hammer
A monarch perched.
Its petal wings flexed
In measured calisthenic.

"No,"
He spread his arms…
"Look."

I turned,
Knelt on the plank
And
Looked.

The roof was sprouting
A garden.
An aureate carpet of spread
Then softly scissoring wings…

Our eyes surely blinked,
But
In honor of the moment
We were motionless...silent.

The golden arrival
Had been a sporadic sprinkling sparkle.
A prescient cascade of coming leaf fall,
And though they lingered long...
A half an hour or so...
The departure was uniformly sudden.

A blanket of wings,
More than a thousand wings,
In what seemed
One downward collective flap
Lifted off in near formation
And flew south.

Their ascent was
Of,
Not into,
Air.

The kid looked at me.
"Did ja feel that?"
I nodded.

None would believe us, but
Against cables and concrete,
Our Island had,
Ever so gently,
Tugged South.

FLOWER GIRLS

Clover...tufted red and white.
Daisy...snowy tresses, a yellow pill box.
Susan...golden black eyed.
Queen Anne...lacy umbel to the sun.

In measured steps,
Spring to fall,
In gay parade they rise,
Sway across my meadow,
And flourish for
A fluttered procession of
Bright winged Royals...

The Tawny Emperor,
His Eastern Tiger,
A Monarch, and
A Viceroy...

To light upon spread petals
And summer sip.

A HAWK AND CROWS

Mark Twain Recalled:

A vast hawk
"Hanging motionless in the sky…
Wings spread wide…
The blue of the vault showing
Through the fringe of end-feathers."

And

Crows
"Perfect gentleman, in deportment and attire…
Not noisy…
Except when holding…conventions in a tree."

Outside Twain's Hartford home,
My son and I stand under
A raucous choir of…
Perfect gentlemen convened
Atop a leafless lattice of sycamore.

On a branch below,
A motionless hawk
No longer vast
With feathers furled.
The prey, awaits.

We stay beneath,
Till, the Murder dispersed.
Free of the mob,
The hawk labors
skyward,

And

Wings spread wide…
The blue of the vault showing
Through the fringe of end-feathers…

Glides above and stoops a solitary crow.

FLIGHT

She flew
Lunar lit;
Windswept hair,
Spinning spokes a-sparkle,
Carefree feet
On peddles aligned
In downhill coast.

She felt,
Maybe heard,
A feathered flutter
In the side-long rush of air.
A shared glance
Eyes a-glint
In downhill flight…

She saw,
Brighter than the moon,
An owl, talons tucked,
Snowy wing tip on her shoulder…
Sidewise Spirit Guide?
Or joy ride…?
Which…mattered not.

SPRING FULL CYCLE...

As first redbuds are in bloom,
chickens lead on leash,
my dog close at heel,
we breathe deep and...
venture vernal.

We breathe deep and...
venture vernal.
my dog close at heel
chickens lead on leash...
as first redbuds are in bloom.

...HARMONIC MOTION

FIRST FLORA

In snow-ringed tree wells
Ephemerals bloom

Sunshine
Absorbed and reflected
Yellow...
Bright white...
In bloodroot, and dandelion.

Too cold for
Bees or butterflies...

Only flies,
Color blind, are
Drawn to pollinate

Sunshine
Absorbed and reflected
Yellow...
Bright white...
In buttercup and starflower.

Spring branch tips
Are
A warm finger smudge
Of
Winter-drawn pencil lines
On
A linen grey sketch pad sky

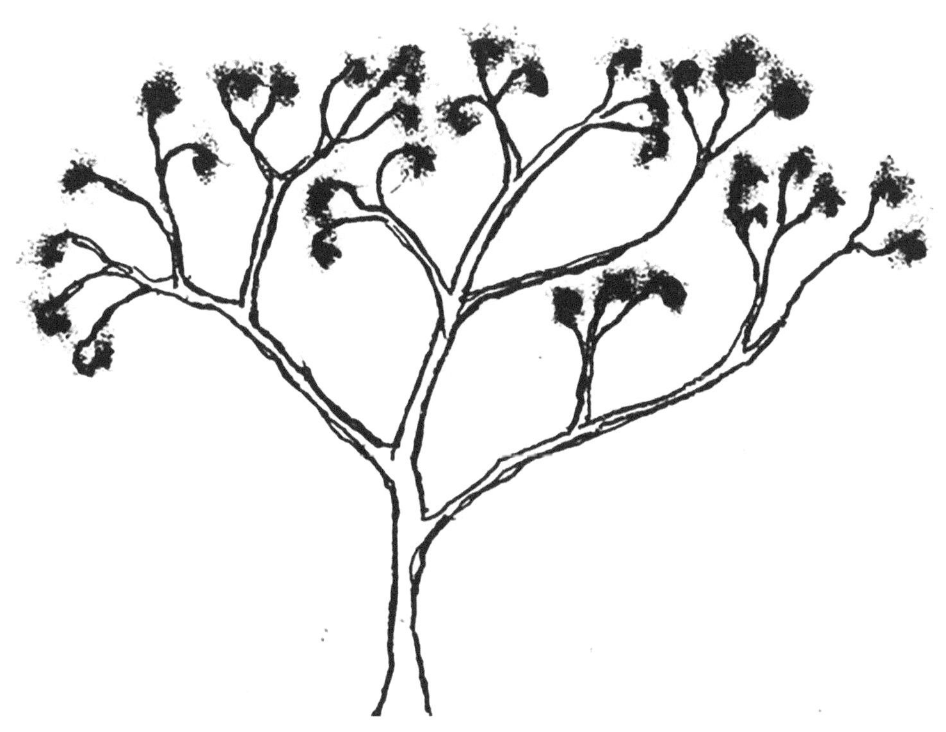

The high bushes are dotted blue...

Each morning a handful

I pick.

Soon,

A harvest wish would be...

Your upturned palms to fill.

SONG OF THE TAWNY THRUSH

Pan's pipes
found in the woods.

Twin voiced…Syrinx…
in assonance echoes
spring songs sung
to returning swallows.

The Veery's lilt
Fills abandoned hollows.

On a low tide beach,
back from a wave tossed swim,
She drips
into her slick mirror image…
shimmers there and casts
a shadow to the dry beyond.
One dog swam.
Three returned.

AUTUMNAL TUMBLE

Woolen boulders,

Shadowed crimp,

Deep-fleeced for coming cold.

Smut-face-blackface-whiteface

Heads a-graze,

Rams and dams browse

Orchard grass and clover.

CONCURRENT EVENTS

THE PREY 11.22.63

With an upward glance…
Saarinen's Black Rock: concrete grid;
Blue-white sparks in dark voids…
Art school friends and I,
Leave sun-splashed West 53rd

For MOMA walls dappled, too.

Hans Hoffman's brightly layered patches,
Splats and strokes of mostly pure pigment,
Lumen Natural…Deliriously Pink, or
A Whisper of the South Wind.

On a gift shop TV, the world stopped
turning.

    CBS NEWS

    CBS NEWS

    CBS NEWS BULLETIN

    CBS NEWS

    CBS NEWS

Dotted gray, Walter Cronkite reports:

Fish in a barrel…
In a specially built car…
Two priests, Dan Rather, and government
Sources say…
Glasses slowly off…
The flash…apparently official…

The Prey:

Hoffman's suspended raven spits down.
The target gyres outward,
Blood smear-smudges.
The blue earth falls away.

The Sun hits the street.

PRESIDENT SHOT DEAD

At the CBS corner,
Twine-bound stacks are tossed.
Unbundled, the banner rises;
Word up from the street…
Welding torches, floor by floor,
Blink to black.

THUNDER FROM THE HEIGHTS
9/10 AND 9/11, 2001

Those days in Portland we lived
Just above the final meander
To the Fore River Falls
And
A bit North of the Jetport.

Friends would ask:
"How can you live there?"

With a raised eye frown,
We would aver:
"It is leafy and green,
And the river is beautiful.

Oh…
The Jetport…the noise?

There really isn't much traffic.

Late at night,
Three Jets deadhead
And leave in the morning.
The prop commuters warm at dawn.

We don't hear it anymore.

People come and go.
No idea who or why,
But they are quiet, too."

On that Tuesday in September,
A mile away,
Mohamed Atta and Abdul al-Omari
Arrived and quietly
Checked into The Comfort Inn.

"Mohamed, we drove from Boston
And return tomorrow for our final flight.
Why the back and forth?"

"Longfellow's home is here…
And before we rise to our destiny,
At Our mezzo cammin…our half way point,
I must spend a moment where the poet penned our prophecy:

Lying beneath me with its sounds and sights,—
  A city in the twilight dim and vast,
With smoking roofs, soft bells, and gleaming lights,—
  And hear above me on the autumnal blast
The cataract of Death far thundering from the heights.

And our epiphany:

And borne aloft by the sustaining blast,
  This little golden thread
Dilates into a column high and vast,
  A form of fear and dread.

Tonight, we buy a box cutter,
Eat pizza
And
Sleep before we soar."

Above the languid stream,
We slept and did not hear
USAir 5930

Wind its props and fly off

To connect

With American 11 in Boston
And, at the tip of Manhattan,
With the North Tower…
A column high and vast.

WATERCOLOR WORKSHOP 2019

I see Mount Blanc...
A white mantled peak still growing...
Human embroidery quaintly dots the terraced skirts below.

I came to paint but cannot pick up my brush.
Farther away:
Green jungles char.
Azure seas writhe in plastic discharge.
Crimson blasts rocket away the weak.

As it scripts the landscape, humankind
Surrounds and sullies the natural palette
And punctuates a stark text with two asterisks.

The first hazily proclaims the underlying, undeniable truth:
"This, too, shall pass."

The second, indelibly inked, mutely cries:
"Too soon."

The quaint chalet patchwork palette will molder.
And nature will find a way forward.
Trees will reclaim deforested meadows.
Mount Blanc will continue to extrude skyward.

If berries and charcoal are foraged,
Survivors will start over,
Find caves beneath the glaciers,
And leave handprint paintings
Of the belled cows that once roamed
The embroidered skirt.

Where did I put my brush?

DEGREES OF SEPARATION
5.25.2020

Long ago,
in the '50s, '60s, And...
just yesterday, I was told:
the Blacks should not complain,
slavery ended long ago.

I thought for a moment.

My great grandmother,
born in 1853,
lived for 100 years.

At 8 or 9, I sat on her lap.
And she told me that perched upon
her father's, she craned her neck
And...
saw Abraham Lincoln,
cocked her ear
And...
heard him say:

"In due time
the weight would be lifted
from the shoulders of all men."

She, no longer on her father's knee,
recalled a bobbing sea of top hats,
and The Great Emancipator.

I, far removed from hers,
Saw George Floyd die,
And...
In an eonic moment of due time,
Heard him...
No longer a slave...
Address his killer as "Sir."

WINDMILLS
12.22.2019

We crossed through Kansas

And as Sancho Panza once had,

"Discovered thirty or forty windmills in that plain."

A welcome slope-sown wave,

Sprouted from a wonderous seed.

Not

As vainglorious Don Q accused,

from a "...wicked ..." one.

Gone mad, the current Don

Glanced, again, at the solar eclipse

And

From beneath his visor of wind-tossed hair confessed:

"I never understood wind."

Yet, somehow,

He knows windmills "very much."

And that

"A windmill will kill many bald eagles."

We rode in their gentle slip stream

And,

with a shake of our heads, echoed Sancho:

"God help us…They were just windmills, and

only a person who had windmills in his head

could fail to realize it?"

COLTSFOOT
APRIL 2020

Thorny microbes float and in stasis stick.

Masked, hands washed, we wait.

Regardless…

At the edge of my woods, Spring emerges.

DO NOT WORRY
11.6.2024

Race over…Racism wins.

Rest assured…your puppies and kittens are safe.

Sextant overboard…Sexism wins.

Unaborted, the good ship Misein Gynē sails to fertile shores.

Climate unchanged…Denialism wins.

Sharpie tracked storms will douse fires in well raked forests.

Constitution sunk…Tourism wins.

Visit a remnant still afloat in a Boston harbor.

POLYCHROMES:
THEN AND SOMEDAY

The rain had stopped.
Flattened droplets slicked the blacktop,
And pooled along the roadside.

With sparkling eyes and
A smile reflecting in a puddle,
My daughter pointed:

"Daddy, look at the colors!"
"Yeah" …I scoffed…
"STP, Exxon Regular, and 10W-30."

"No! No!"
 She cried out with glee:
"The puddle caught a rainbow!"

Someday it may.

CLOSE ENCOUNTERS

TIME...REEL AND PASSING

At the end of the summer in 1958,
I train into the City with a date.
We cuddle together at a matinee
in a Times Square movie house.

The Young Lions.

I have read the book,
and she loves Brando.

After the flick, hand in hand,
we return to Grand Central
to catch a train home.

We enter on the upper level
puzzled.

On the towered golden clock
the big and little hands have spun
two hours ahead.

In real time,
we a share shrug,
wrinkle of our brows,
and move on.

At the top of the stairs
that fan down to the lower level,
we are, again, surprised.

The landing is blocked.
Access to the tracks below is denied...
Velvet ropes and a couple of New York's finest.

I ask one of the cops: "What's up?"

With a sideways tilt of his head
and a flip of his thumb,
he gestures below.

"Hitchcock's making a movie."

I peer around the gold-buttoned, blue bulk in front of me
and take in the view beyond. Indeed, off to the left,
perched in a padded seat and raised aloft,
Hitchcock in well-known profile,
floats into view.

Down and farther to the left,
next to a phone booth
and reflected in polished parquet,
distinguished in a blue gray suit,
Cary Grant awaits direction.

Caught up in a moment,
two hours ahead in an improbable time,
we move around the balcony
to an over the railing vantage point
directly above Grant and what appears,
in this time and place,
to be his phone booth.

Hitchcock waves his hand.

I don't hear "Action."
I guess, with him,
a flourish of the hand is enough.

On gestured cue, Cary
ducks into the phone booth.

Seconds later, he emerges,
hurries diagonally across the station floor,
pauses only for a double take
at a man standing reading a newspaper,
and strides on to merge with a crowd of
extras milling around the far-side ticket windows.

Two hours into a cinematic future and
any time *North by Northwest* plays on a TV
or at some Hitchcock themed film festival…
then and now…she and I,
agog, on tiptoes, are there
and fifteen forever.

A FILM REEL CHATTERS
BRIGHT MOMENTS ON A WIDE SCREEN…
TECHNICOLOR TIME WARP.

IT'S MAGIC

Stiff armed,
Across the sideline,
I sprawled face first.

I blinked my eyes
Shook clumped turf
From my faceguard

And...blinked again at...

My face mirrored on
The tapered tip of a
Black high-heeled shoe.

My gaze, instep to calf,
Rose to the shimmering hem
Of a black fur coat.

I came to my feet.
Her coat coned open
And held a golden face.

Black fur pillbox,
A blond page boy,
Blue eyes and red lips...

I shyly smiled.
She winked,
Clapped once and smiled, too.

In 1960...
A bit out of bounds...
On a High School football field,
I had my Doris Day.

BERMUDA... CHAPTER TWO

The Chapter Two film crew was late.
But in the St. George town square,
The stars were aligned.

Spotlit by noonday sun and
About to play the role of herself,
Marsha Mason dazzled.

James Caan paced the cobbles,
Tossed a tiny lariat,
And lassoed things small and stationary.

My sister wanted to be an Extra.
Fingers crossed,
I hoped she would be.

Caan was bored and so was I.
He headed for the White Horse Tavern.
I followed him and straddled an adjacent stool.

We ordered Heinekens,
And in long swallows knocked them back.
The tiny rope twirled just above the bar rail.

"Hey," I asked, "Catch anything out there?"
He said, "Nope," pocketed the rope,
Drained his beer and swiveled away.

I turned to watch him go.
My sister, eyes agleam,
Shook her head and patted my back.

She needed something
Extra...
I gave her his coaster.

With a frown
She rolled her eyes and asked:
"Couldn't get your pal to sign it?"

BENEDETTO

Stuck in LaGuardia…
Thunderstorms in Atlanta…
No one is flying the friendly skies.

A pass the time, beer in hand,
I look for a place to sit.
The bar is full.

I spot a seat at one of those
tiny precariously stooled
tables for two.

The guy seated
is nursing a cold one
and gently humming.

"If you can find it in your heart,
may I join you?"
He nods.

"Anything goes.
This is the good life, and
you're just in time."

He croons on…
"The best is yet to come.
Are you havin' any fun?"

"Because of you,
I have a place to sit.
Where you headed?"

"Unless you can
fly me to the moon,
I'll find my heart in San Francisco."

STAR-CROSSED

Again and again and again
My eyes roll back,
I sigh, turn my palms skyward and ask:

What is it with his…
Constant…
Attraction to and praise for
Other women?

Doris…
      Long ago he met her
      In mink coat sparkling?
Katherine…
      Grace from morning glory to
      Golden pond?
Audrey…
      Dream maker…heart breaker
      Finding Cat in the pouring rain?

Hmmm…Could it be that I am
A part of,
Not apart from,
His galaxy of stars?

ILLUSTRATED HAIKUS

Cloud capped mountain

Relentless mist…will wash your

Sky edge to the sea

Bright morning crystal

Dew drop…katsura cupped

I will not drink you

South slope sun sets and

Amber edge firs reach and hold

Day's end…last light left

Green laurel cradles

Cupped snow spoons stretched to

Touch the longer day

A solitary jay…

Blue on winter morning blue…

Flurries branch held snow

As the evening lights

Your path, I will watch over you

Out of your way

Morning frosted rose

Crimson crystal...shatter not

One last warm dawn breaks

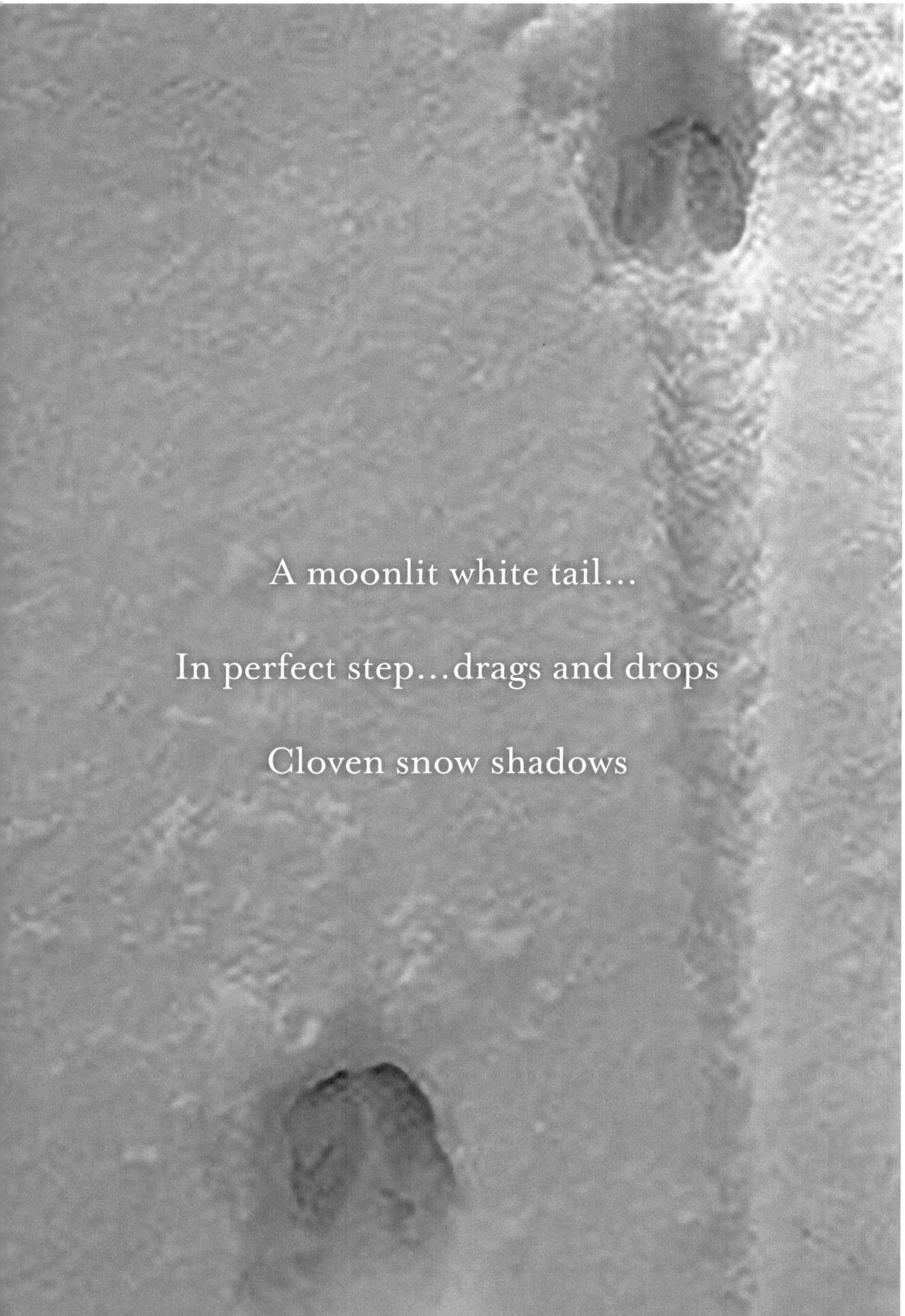

A moonlit white tail…

In perfect step…drags and drops

Cloven snow shadows

Wolf moon occulted

Mars…Mars spins free. I orbit

Renewed at eighty-two

Spring maple flower...

Viridescent veils

Promise...summer shade

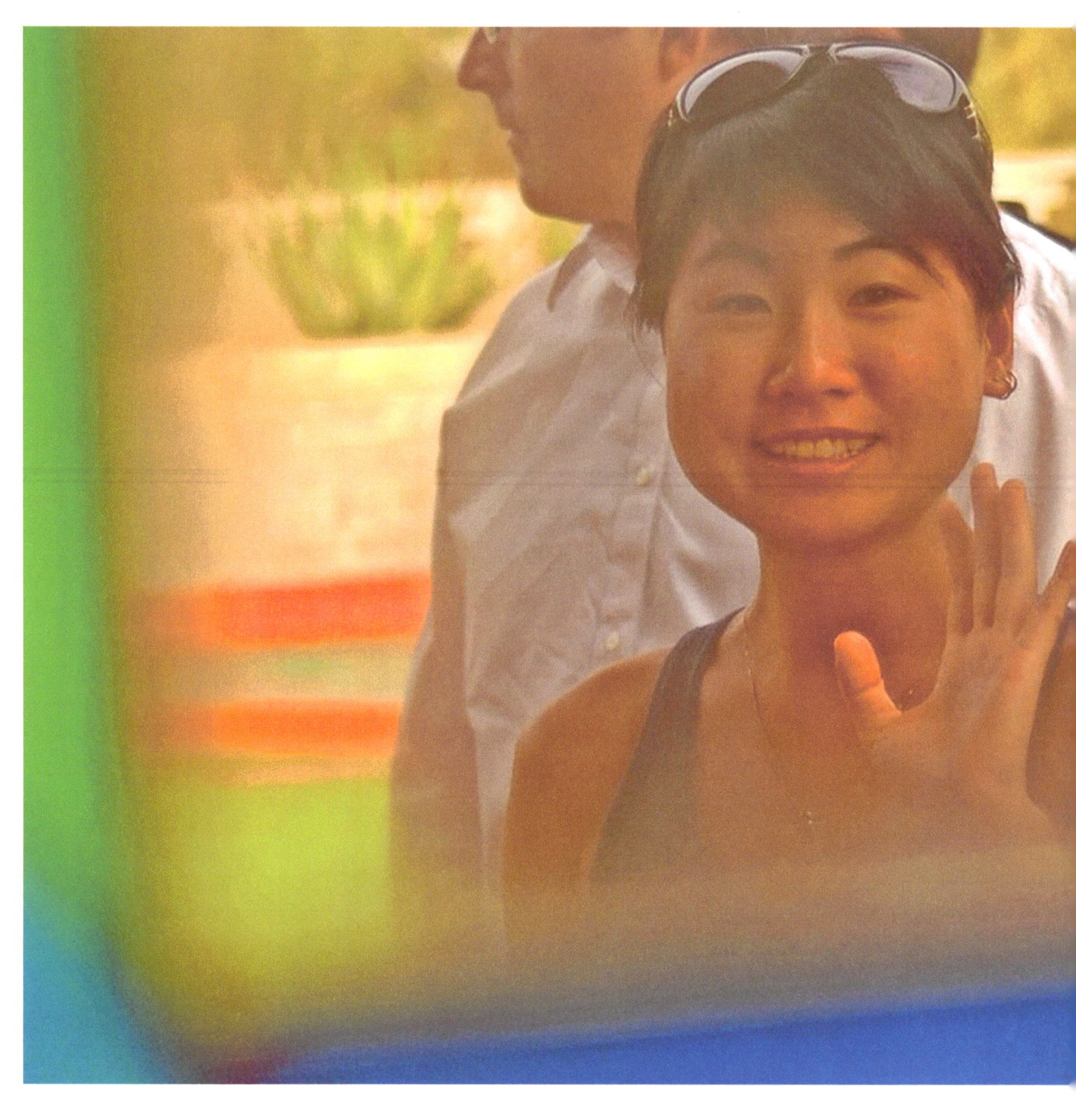

Reflected, she waves

Behind me, a room away

We share...mirror world

Today, one inch square,

The flakes are postage stamps...

Snow arrives air mail

Cubs low, mama high

Black bears snack my peaches, and…

Kindly…leave me one

From sun warmed shores,

A fall tied fly cast over

A rainbow eddy

Sumi-e brushed sky...

A calligraphy of geese

ink a southward script

I will care for you

We can wander deep green places

If we just hold hands

CLOSING THOUGHTS

CORRECTED VISION

Blurry in the here and now,
I imagine time travel
to an eye appointment in Philly.
Medicare covers it.
And
Ben Franklin fixes my bifocals.

Here and now...
Lenses brand new...
I can look long and read up close.

Close up...and by my shoulder...
On shelves of 'Take One/Leave One' books,
I clearly see Shirley MacLaine smiling.
In bright white,
Eyes upcast and her face held by
Trouble with Harry hair,
She descends cross-legged
From a star filled sky.

She smiles. She sees. She shares...
Asks: What If and leads me to
Radiant other worlds.

What If,
I had looked
The other way?

Vision enhanced,
To those shelves I will return
And leave a book.
But...
Not this one.

THEN AND NOW

Over time, with

Keys lost

and

Combinations jumbled,

Memory banks,

Once safe storage,

Breech and spill our

Past into the current:

A meandering stream

Of unbound, erosive edges.

Now with love as levee, let us

Live and remember...

As best we can.

HETERONYMS
AND HOMONYMS

Words…can
Affect my affect.

On a walk in the woods…
A moment of renewal…
I recreate to recreate.

And hope, in recreation,
I have learned to be
More learned.

Wind will wind through
Gilded leaf light.
This autumn I will…

Play on words
And not Fall
On my sword

SECOND THOUGHTS

Cain, not his brother's,
Kills the Keeper of the Flock
And…

God sends
A flood to drown
The sorrow of His creation
But…

Allows the Ark.

The waters recede.
Noah's zoo begets,
And…

The spawn of Cain
Kill the Keepers of the Flocks,
And…

God sends

A gradual warming;
A slow flood with no Noah,
And…

God ends

The sorrow of His creation.

SHADOWS AND REFLECTIONS

Reflecting in the shadows

Of a roofless building,

A half-filled bottle

Props open a sash with no glass

And...

Lets in fresh air.